Favorite TRADITIONAL QUILTS
Made Easy

JO PARROTT

Martingale®
& COMPANY

Favorite Traditional Quilts Made Easy
© 2008 by Jo Parrott

That Patchwork Place® is an imprint of
Martingale & Company®.

Martingale & Company
20205 144th Ave. NE
Woodinville, WA 98072-8478 USA
www.martingale-pub.com

Printed in China
13 12 11 10 09 08   8 7 6 5 4 3 2 1

Library of Congress Cataloging-in-Publication Data
Library of Congress Control Number: 2008027492

ISBN: 978-1-56477-843-7

CREDITS

President & CEO: Tom Wierzbicki
Publisher: Jane Hamada
Editorial Director: Mary V. Green
Managing Editor: Tina Cook
Technical Editor: Nancy Mahoney
Copy Editor: Marcy Heffernan
Design Director: Stan Green
Production Manager: Regina Girard
Illustrator: Adrienne Smitke
Cover & Text Designer: Adrienne Smitke
Photographer: Brent Kane

❖ MISSION STATEMENT ❖

Dedicated to providing quality products
and service to inspire creativity.

Dedication

*To all my quilting sisters everywhere, especially
the quilters from Country Junction Quilt Store
in Wills Point, Texas, and the Heritage
Quilt Guild of Van Zandt County*

      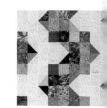

Contents

Introduction

I've been quilting for 25 years now, sewing for over 60 years, and my philosophy hasn't changed much. I like to make pretty things as fast as I can.

In June 1982, my sewing preferences changed when I took my first quilting class. The entire quilt was handmade, no sewing machine involved, and it took until September to complete the project. As much as I enjoyed making the quilt, I felt sure there had to be an easier and/or faster way. In the next 18 months, I took 12 more classes; most were strip- or speed-piecing classes.

One of my greatest joys, besides my 23 grandchildren and 10 great grandchildren, is bringing my style of quiltmaking to new quilters. Beginner quilters are so much fun. I also like to take patterns that have different angles, and at one time required weird-shaped templates, and make them easier to piece. The Hunter's Star and Pineapple block projects in this book are quilts I've worked with over the years until I got them how I wanted them—beautiful quilts that I can teach beginners to make.

Color in quilting is such an individual thing. I like bright fabrics and strong contrasts. After taking a color class, I decided that what I needed to know and remember was which colors were complementary to each other. And that works for me. I find if I like the fabric, the quilt is so much easier and quicker to make.

It's been a pleasure seeing the evolution of quilting, which continues to grow and spread, kind of like a family tree. There are many branches and many ways to make a quilt. We in quiltmaking are so lucky to be able to "do our own thing." There is a place for everyone. So find your place; make and experiment with quilts and fabric. It's cheaper (well maybe) than a psychologist and way more fun!

Keep on quilting!

The special techniques described here are designed for accuracy and speed in making quilts—the two things I consider most important. Spend some time reading these instructions and you will increase your enjoyment of making quilts.

ACCURATE CUTTING AND SEWING

Two important aspects of machine piecing are accuracy in cutting and sewing an accurate ¼" seam allowance. This enables seams to match and the pieces to fit together properly. The finished block size is the most important measurement. If a finished block size is 12", then all of the blocks should be 12". The following is a test to help you make adjustments in your sewing so you can achieve an accurate ¼"-wide seam allowance.

1. Cut one 1½"-wide strip across the width of fabric (selvage to selvage). Crosscut the strip into six pieces measuring 1½" x 4½" and one piece measuring 1½" x 6½". Sew the 4½" pieces together in pairs as shown.

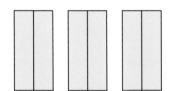

2. Sew the pairs together to make one 4½" x 6½" rectangle. Press all seam allowances in one direction.

3. Sew the 1½" x 6½" piece to the top of the rectangle from step 2. It should be an exact fit. Press the seam allowance toward the last piece added. The rectangle should now measure 5½" x 6½".

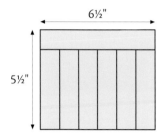

4. If the 6½" piece is too long, that means the seam allowances between the 4½" pieces are too wide. If the 6½" piece is too short, then the seam allowances between the 4½" pieces are too narrow. Cut another 1½"-wide strip and repeat steps 1–3, adjusting the ¼" seam allowance as needed, so that the set of 4½" pieces and the 6½" piece fit together exactly. I can't emphasis enough the need for an accurate ¼" seam allowance.

HALF-SQUARE-TRIANGLE GRID TECHNIQUE

This technique is one that has been in and out of favor for the last 25 years. I use it when I need to make a lot of half-square-triangle units quickly. You will need two fabric pieces the size given in the cutting directions for the project you are making. You'll also need a 17" x 23" (or larger) rotary-cutting mat, a 24"-long ruler with ⅛" marks, a non-smearing ballpoint pen, and a sharp pencil. And of course, a rotary cutter and sewing machine.

1. Center the two fabric pieces, right sides together, on the cutting mat. Once the fabric is placed on the mat *do not* move it again until you're ready to start sewing. On one end of the fabric, align your ruler with the first vertical line on the mat and using a non-smearing pen,

draw a straight line on the wrong side of the top fabric. You'll use the non-smearing pen for steps 1–5.

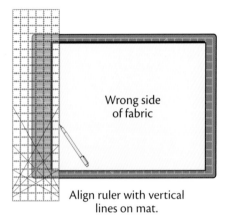

Align ruler with vertical lines on mat.

Why a Non-Smearing Pen?

I like using a non-smearing ballpoint pen because it moves easily over the fabric. You can tell if it's non-smearing by making a line on a piece of paper and wiping your finger across it. If you don't have a non-smearing pen, you can use a permanent ink pen.

2. Using the lines on your ruler and measuring from the first drawn line, draw vertical lines as specified in the project instructions. This should be the desired finished size plus ⅞". For example, for a 2" finished square, the lines would be 2⅞" apart.

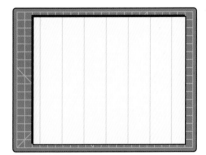

Draw vertical lines.

3. Turn the mat as needed, without moving or picking up the fabric. On one end of the fabric, align your ruler with the first horizontal line

on the mat and draw a straight line. Then using the lines on your ruler and measuring from the first drawn line, draw horizontal lines to complete a grid.

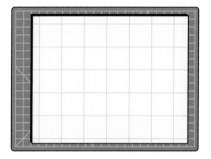

Draw horizontal lines to complete the grid.

4. Draw a diagonal line from corner to corner in each square as shown, skipping every other square. These lines are drawn from the upper left to the lower right.

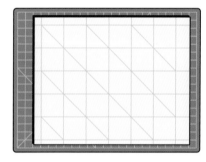

Draw diagonal lines in one direction.

5. In the remaining squares, draw a diagonal line from corner to corner as shown. These lines are drawn from the upper right to the lower left. All squares in the grid should have one diagonal line. All diagonal lines should go through the corner of the drawn squares. The pen lines will be the cutting lines.

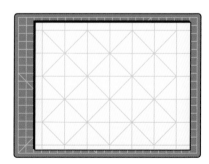

Finish drawing diagonal lines.

6. Now use a sharp pencil to draw a ¼" line on *both sides* of every diagonal line as shown. The pencil lines are your sewing lines.

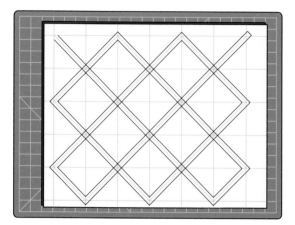

Draw sewing lines.

7. Place pins where the vertical and horizontal lines cross to hold the two fabric pieces together for sewing. Now you can pick up the fabrics from the mat.

Following the Arrows

At first glance, the diagram after step 8 can look a bit confusing. Before you start sewing, I recommend using the eraser end of a pencil to trace the arrows on your fabric piece; this will help you see the path of the continuous seam. You'll follow the red arrows first, and then follow the green arrows. When sewing, stop with your needle in the down position at a horizontal or vertical line, pivot the fabric, and continue sewing. You will need to sew or "travel" outside the grid lines as you follow the green arrows. The continuous seam is what makes this technique work so well.

8. Begin at the upper-left corner and sew on all the pencil lines. Sew one continuous seam until all of the pencil diagonal lines have been stitched. Make sure you sew on both sides of the diagonal pen lines. Remove the pins.

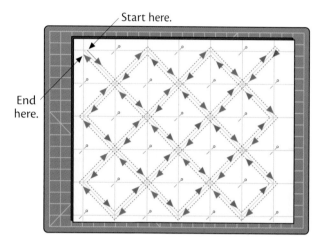

9. Press the sewn grid to set the seams before cutting. Place the sewn grid on a cutting mat and *do not* move it until all cutting has been completed. Trim away the excess fabric outside the grid drawing. Cut all vertical pen lines, cut all horizontal pen lines, and finally cut all diagonal pen lines. Each square will make two half-square-triangle units. Press the seam allowances toward the color indicated in the project instructions. Measure each pressed half-square-triangle unit to make sure it is the correct size for the project you are making. This should be the desired finished size plus ½".

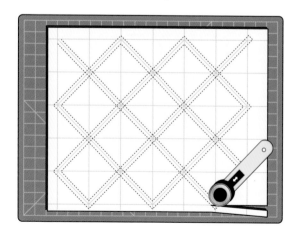

SCRAP HALF-SQUARE-TRIANGLE UNITS

I use this method for making half-square-triangle units when I want a scrappy look or only need a few units.

1. Cut the squares ⅞" larger than the desired finished size of the half-square-triangle unit. The size to cut is given in each of the project cutting directions. Separate into stacks of light squares and dark squares.

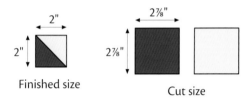

Finished size

Cut size

2. Using a sharp pencil and a ruler, draw a diagonal line from corner to corner on the wrong side of the light fabric. Then draw a line ¼" on each side of the first diagonal line as shown; these will be your sewing lines.

Mark lines.

3. Layer the squares right sides together in pairs, with the light color on top of the darker color. Stitch on each side of the center diagonal line, sewing on the marked lines. Cut the squares apart on the center diagonal line. Press the seam allowances toward the darker fabric to yield two half-square-triangle units.

Assembly-Line Stitching

I like to assembly-line (or chain) stitch the squares together. To do this, I sew the first pair of squares together, stitching on the marked line on one side of the center diagonal line, and then without lifting the presser foot or cutting the thread, I sew the next pair of squares together. When I've stitched 10 or 12 pairs of squares, I clip the thread after the last pair and remove the pieces from the machine. I don't clip the thread between the squares yet. Then, I feed the squares under the presser foot again, this time sewing on the marked line on the other side of the center diagonal line. After sewing the last piece, I clip the threads, cutting the squares apart.

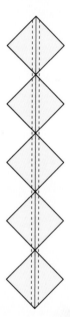

Sew ¼" from center line.

CORNER TRIANGLES

Several of the quilts in this book feature blocks made with this speedy technique. This is a simple way to create triangle shapes without actually cutting triangles or sewing on a bias-cut edge, and it gives neat and accurate results. This technique starts with a square.

1. Cut the squares ½" larger than the desired finished size of the half-square triangle. The size to cut is given in each of the project cutting directions. Using a sharp pencil and a ruler, draw a diagonal line from corner to corner on the wrong side of the square as directed.

Mark line.

2. With right sides together, position the squares on the larger square, rectangle, or unit as directed in the quilt instructions and pin as shown. Make sure the diagonal line is pointing in the correct direction, and then stitch on the drawn line. After sewing a few stitches, stop and realign the square if needed. Once the seam is complete, remove the pin.

Pin and stitch.

3. Use a sharp pair of scissors to trim away the outer corner of the square, cutting ¼" from the stitching line. *Do not* trim away any of the bottom layer (square, rectangle, or unit). Keeping

the bottom layer intact will help stabilize the corner and keep your piece square. Flip open the top square of fabric and press to complete the corner triangle. If the corner triangle extends beyond the bottom layer, trim the sides of the triangle even with the bottom layer.

 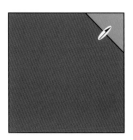

Trim.   Press.

PRESSING

In machine piecing, pressing can be your best friend. Unlike hand piecing, which leaves a loose seam allowance intersection that can be pressed in either direction as needed, with machine piecing you need to decide as the block is assembled which direction the seam allowance will lie. It should also be noted that the seam allowance should be pressed, *not ironed*.

To avoid distorting quilt pieces, be sure to press carefully by lifting and then lowering your iron onto the pieces without moving the iron from side to side. Place the piece that the seam allowance is to be pressed toward on the top, and then use the tip of the iron to gently push the fabric over the seam allowance. Always press the seam allowances in the desired direction from the front or right side of the block. This will help eliminate pleats and tucks. Press the seam allowances in the direction indicated by the arrows in the project illustrations unless otherwise noted.

Purple Passion Pineapple Quilt

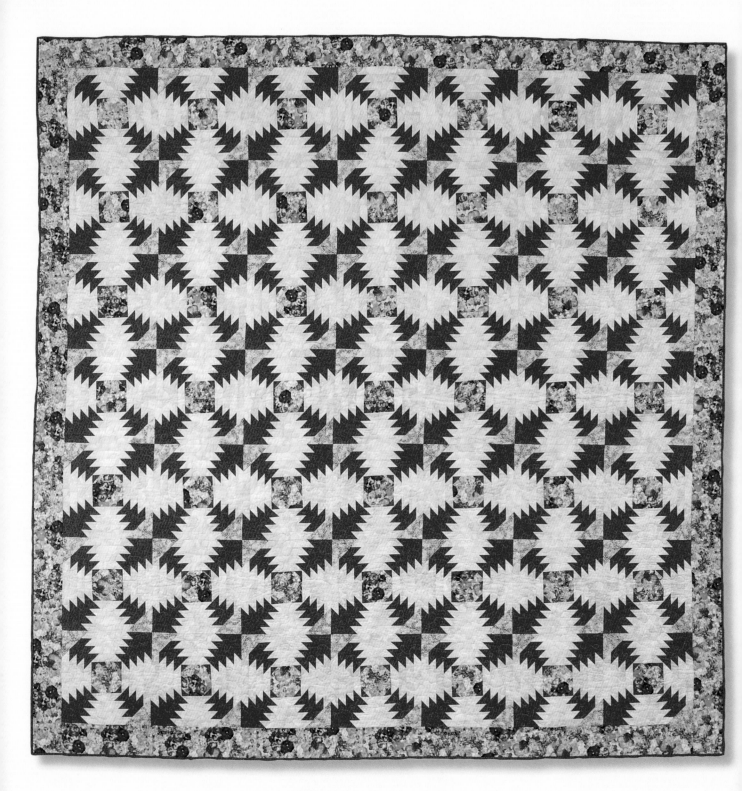

Pieced and quilted by Jo Parrott

The Pineapple is a favorite block that can be made using several different techniques. The problem with most techniques is that the blocks aren't always the same finished size, which makes assembly difficult. Quick-and-easy techniques are only good when they yield straight and square blocks. In the following method, you'll cut strips the size needed, thus making blocks the correct size. As always, an accurate seam allowance is essential.

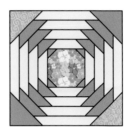

Finished quilt: 94½" x 94½"
Finished block: 12"

MATERIALS

All yardages are based on 42"-wide fabric.
8⅜ yards of background fabric for blocks
6¾ yards of purple tone-on-tone print for blocks
    and binding
2⅞ yards of floral print for block centers and border
1⅓ yards of small-scale print for blocks
9¼ yards of fabric for backing
100" x 100" piece of batting

CUTTING

All measurements include ¼"-wide seam allowances.
Cut all strips across the width of the fabric (selvage to selvage). Read all the directions before starting, referring to "Special Techniques" on page 7 as needed.

From the floral print, cut:
10 strips, 5½" x 42"
7 strips, 4½" x 42"; crosscut into 49 squares,
    4½" x 4½"

From the purple tone-on-tone print, cut:
10 strips, 4" x 42"; crosscut into 98 squares, 4" x 4"
18 strips, 3½" x 42"; crosscut into 196 squares,
    3½" x 3½"
16 strips, 3" x 42"; crosscut into 196 squares,
    3" x 3"
13 strips, 2½" x 42"; crosscut into 196 squares,
    2½" x 2½"
8 strips, 1½" x 42"; crosscut into 196 squares,
    1½" x 1½"
10 binding strips, 2½" x 42"

From the background fabric, cut:
4 strips, 12½" x 42"; crosscut into 98 rectangles,
    1½" x 12½"
8 strips, 10½" x 42"; crosscut into 196 rectangles,
    1½" x 10½"
8 strips, 8½" x 42"; crosscut into 196 rectangles,
    1½" x 8½"
8 strips, 6½" x 42"; crosscut into 196 rectangles,
    1½" x 6½"
4 strips, 4½" x 42"; crosscut into 98 rectangles,
    1½" x 4½"

From the small-scale print, cut:
10 strips, 4" x 42"; crosscut into 98 squares, 4" x 4"

Making the Blocks

Refer to "Corner Triangles" on page 11 for details.

1. Draw a diagonal line from corner to corner on the wrong side of each 1½" purple square. Place a marked square on each corner of a 4½" floral square, right sides together. Sew on the diagonal lines.

2. Trim away the outer corner of the purple squares, leaving the bottom layer intact. Flip open the remaining purple triangles and press. Make 49 center units.

Make 49.

3. Sew 1½" x 4½" background rectangles to opposite sides of the center unit. Press the seam allowances toward the background fabric.

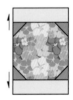

4. Sew 1½" x 6½" background rectangles to the remaining sides of the center unit. Press the seam allowances toward the background fabric. Do not trim away any part of the background strips. They should be an exact fit; if not, check your seam allowance. This will keep your block square. The units should measure 6½" x 6½", which includes seam allowances. Make 49 units.

Make 49.

5. Draw a diagonal line from corner to corner on the wrong side of each 2½" purple square. Place a marked square on each corner of a center unit from step 4. Sew on the diagonal lines. Trim away the outer corner of the purple squares, leaving the bottom layer intact. Flip open the remaining purple triangles and press. Make 49 units.

Make 49.

6. Sew 1½" x 6½" background rectangles to opposite sides of the unit from step 5. Press the seam allowances toward the background fabric.

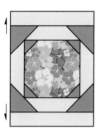

7. Sew 1½" x 8½" background rectangles to the remaining sides of the unit. Press the seam allowances toward the background fabric. Make 49 units.

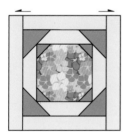

Make 49.

14

8. Repeat steps 5, 6, and 7, adding pieces in the following order:
   - Four 3" purple squares
   - Two 1½" x 8½" background rectangles
   - Two 1½" x 10½" background rectangles
   - Four 3½" purple squares
   - Two 1½" x 10½" background rectangles
   - Two 1½" x 12½" background rectangles

9. Draw a diagonal line from corner to corner on the wrong side of each 4" small-scale print square. Place a marked square on opposite corners of each unit. Sew on the diagonal lines; trim and press.

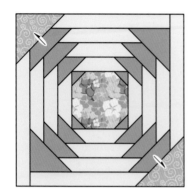

10. Draw a diagonal line from corner to corner on the wrong side of each 4" purple square. Place a marked square on the remaining corners of each unit. Sew on the diagonal lines; trim and press. Each block should measure 12½" x 12½", which includes seam allowances. Make 49 Pineapple blocks.

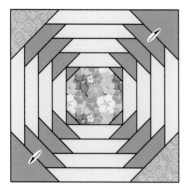

Make 49.

ASSEMBLING AND FINISHING THE QUILT

1. Arrange the blocks in seven rows of seven blocks each, as shown in the quilt assembly diagram below.

2. Sew the blocks into rows. Press the seam allowances in alternate directions from row to row. Sew the rows together. Press the seam allowances in one direction.

3. Refer to "Adding Borders" on page 43. Measure, cut, and sew the 5½"-wide floral strips to the quilt top for the outer border. Press all seam allowances toward the newly added border.

4. Layer the quilt with batting and the pieced backing; baste. Hand or machine quilt as desired.

5. Refer to "Binding Your Quilt" on page 44 and use the 2½"-wide purple strips to bind the quilt.

Quilt assembly

15

Pieced and quilted by Jo Parrott

This Pineapple block table runner pattern is designed for ease in assembly. All the pieces are cut to the exact size needed. No trimming! As long as the cutting and piecing are accurate, everything will go together perfectly. Have fun!

Finished size: 17" x 51"
Finished block: 12"

MATERIALS

All yardages are based on 42"-wide fabric.
1¼ yards of background fabric for blocks and
    setting triangles
½ yard of red floral for blocks
½ yard of green fabric for blocks
1⅓ yards of fabric for backing

CUTTING

All measurements include ¼"-wide seam allowances.
Cut all strips across the width of the fabric (selvage to selvage). Read all the directions before starting, referring to "Special Techniques" on page 7 as needed.

From the red floral, cut:
1 strip, 4½" x 42"; crosscut into 3 squares,
    4½" x 4½"
2 strips, 4" x 42"; crosscut into 12 squares, 4" x 4"

From the green fabric cut:
2 strips, 3½" x 42"; crosscut into 12 squares,
    3½" x 3½"
1 strip, 3" x 42"; crosscut into 12 squares, 3" x 3"
1 strip, 2½" x 42"; crosscut into 12 squares,
    2½" x 2½"
1 strip, 1½" x 42"; crosscut into 12 squares,
    1½" x 1½"

From the background fabric cut:
12 strips, 1½" x 42"; crosscut into:
   • 6 rectangles, 1½" x 12½"
   • 12 rectangles, 1½" x 10½"
   • 12 rectangles, 1½" x 8½"
   • 12 rectangles, 1½" x 6½"
   • 6 rectangles, 1½" x 4½"
1 square, 18¼" x 18¼"; cut twice diagonally to yield
    4 quarter-square triangles

From the backing fabric, cut:
2 pieces, 20" x 42"

Making the Blocks

Refer to "Corner Triangles" on page 11 for details.

1. Draw a diagonal line from corner to corner on the wrong side of each 1½" green square. Place a marked square on each corner of a 4½" red floral square, right sides together. Sew on the diagonal lines.

2. Trim away the outer corner of the green squares, leaving the bottom layer intact. Flip open the remaining green triangles and press. Make three center units.

Make 3.

3. Sew 1½" x 4½" background rectangles to opposite sides of the center unit. Press the seam allowances toward the background fabric.

4. Sew 1½" x 6½" background rectangles to the remaining sides of the center unit. Press the seam allowances toward the background fabric Do not trim away any part of the background strips. They should be an exact fit; if not, check your seam allowance. This will keep your block square. The units should measure 6½" x 6½", which includes seam allowances. Make three units.

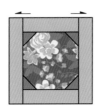

Make 3.

5. Draw a diagonal line from corner to corner on the wrong side of each 2½" green square. Place a marked square on each corner of a center unit from step 4. Sew on the diagonal lines. Trim away the outer corner of the green squares, leaving the bottom layer intact. Flip open the remaining green triangles and press. Make three units.

Make 3.

6. Sew 1½" x 6½" background rectangles to opposite sides of the unit from step 5. Press the seam allowances toward the background fabric.

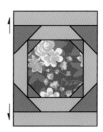

7. Sew 1½" x 8½" background rectangles to the remaining sides of the unit. Press the seam allowances toward the background fabric. Make three units.

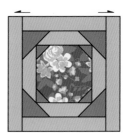

Make 3.

18

8. Repeat steps 5, 6, and 7, adding pieces in the following order:
   - Four 3" green squares
   - Two 1½" x 8½" background rectangles
   - Two 1½" x 10½" background rectangles
   - Four 3½" green squares
   - Two 1½" x 10½" background rectangles
   - Two 1½" x 12½" background rectangles
   - Four 4" red floral squares

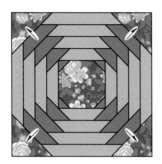

Make 3.

ASSEMBLING AND FINISHING THE TABLE RUNNER

1. Arrange the blocks and the background triangles together in diagonal rows as shown. Sew the blocks and triangles into rows. Press the seam allowances toward the triangles.

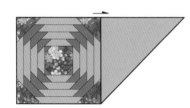

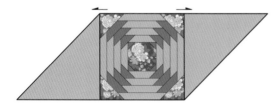

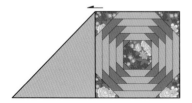

2. Sew the rows together; press.

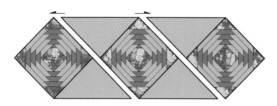

3. Sew the two pieces of backing fabric together, end to end, and press the seam allowance open. Trim the excess fabric so the backing is approximately 20" x 60".

4. Center the table runner on top of the backing, right sides together, and pin in place. Using a ¼"-wide seam allowance, stitch all the way around the outer edge, leaving a 6" opening on one side for turning. Note that there is no batting in this table runner.

Leave open for turning.

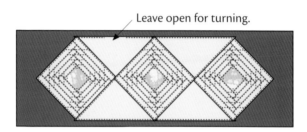

5. Trim the excess backing even with the table runner. Turn the table runner right side out through the opening. Work the seam edges between your thumb and finger and direct the backing slightly to the backside at the seam line; press. Use a blind stitch to sew the opening closed.

6. Topstitch around the outer edge of the table runner. Hand or machine quilt along the seams of the Pineapple blocks to hold the layers together.

Make It Reversible

You can make your table runner reversible by using completely different fabrics to make two table runners. Then instead of using backing fabric, place them right sides together and sew them as described above. Make one side for everyday use and one for a favorite holiday. You can use the table runner twice as often.

Pieced and quilted by Jo Parrott

In the past, the Hunter's Star block was made with oddly shaped templates—a diamond, triangle, and a trapezoid—so it was often easier to hand piece the blocks. The technique I use for this pattern requires only squares and half-square triangles. An easy method for making half-square triangles makes the process even quicker.

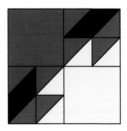

Finished quilt: 66½" x 74½"
Finished block: 8"

MATERIALS

All yardages are based on 42"-wide fabric.
2 yards of fabric A (red) for arrows
2 yards of fabric B (light pink background)
    for arrows
1⅓ yards of fabric C (black) for stars and
    inner border
2⅝ yards of fabric D (pink) for stars, outer border,
    and binding
4⅜ yards of fabric for backing
72" x 80" piece of batting

CUTTING

*All measurements include ¼"-wide seam allowances.
Cut all strips across the width of the fabric (selvage to
selvage). Read all the directions before starting, referring
to "Special Techniques" on page 7 as needed.*

From fabric A, cut:
2 strips, 16" x 42"; crosscut into 4 rectangles,
    16" x 20"
7 strips, 4½" x 42"; crosscut into 56 squares,
    4½" x 4½"

From fabric B, cut:
2 strips, 16" x 42"; crosscut into 4 rectangles,
    16" x 20"
7 strips, 4½" x 42"; crosscut into 56 squares,
    4½" x 4½"

From fabric C, cut:
2 strips, 16" x 42"; crosscut into 4 rectangles,
    16" x 20"
7 strips, 1½" x 42"

From fabric D, cut:
2 strips, 16" x 42"; crosscut into 4 rectangles,
    16" x 20"
7 strips, 4½" x 42"
8 strips, 2½" x 42"

21

Color Swatch

Even though this quilt uses only four fabrics, the fabrics are used in different places in the block, which can become confusing. So, for easy reference, I find it handy to cut a swatch of each of my fabrics and either pin them or paste them with fabric glue to a sheet of paper. I then label each swatch as fabric A, B, C, or D to help me keep on track as I'm cutting and sewing my quilt pieces.

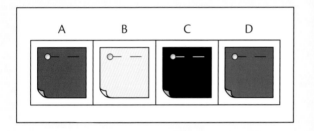

MAKING THE HALF-SQUARE-TRIANGLE UNITS

Refer to "Half-Square-Triangle Grid Technique" on page 7 for details.

1. Layer the 16" x 20" rectangles in pairs, right sides together, with the lighter fabric on top in the following combinations. Make two of each:
   - Fabric A and fabric C
   - Fabric A and fabric B
   - Fabric B and fabric D
   - Fabric C and fabric D

2. Draw a 2⅞" grid on the wrong side of each top rectangle. Sew the rectangles together as described in "Half-Square-Triangle Grid Technique."

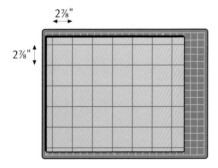

Make 2 of each.

3. Cut on the lines to make 112 half-square-triangle units from each fabric combination. Press the seam allowances toward fabrics A and D. Each half-square-triangle unit should measure 2½" square. (You'll have eight extra half-square-triangle units from each fabric combination for your scrap bag.)

Make 112 of each.

MAKING THE BLOCKS

1. Sew an A/C half-square-triangle unit and a C/D half-square-triangle unit together as shown; press. Make 56 units.

Make 56.

2. Sew an A/B half-square-triangle unit and a D/B half-square-triangle unit together as shown; press. Make 56 units.

Make 56.

3. Sew one unit from step 1 and one unit from step 2 together to make a unit that measures 4½" square; press. Make 56 units.

Make 56.

4. Sew a fabric A square to the left side of each unit from step 3. Press the seam allowances toward fabric A. Make 56 units.

Make 56.

5. Sew an A/C half-square-triangle unit and an A/B half-square-triangle unit together as shown; press. Make 56 units.

Make 56.

6. Sew a C/D half-square-triangle unit and a D/B half-square-triangle unit together as shown; press. Make 56 units.

Make 56.

7. Sew one unit from step 5 and one unit from step 6 together to make a unit that measures 4½" square; press. Make 56 units.

Make 56.

8. Sew a fabric B square to the right side of the unit from step 7. Press the seam allowances toward fabric B. Make 56 units.

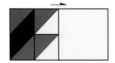

Make 56.

9. Sew one unit from step 4 and one unit from step 8 together as shown to make one block; press. Make 56 blocks.

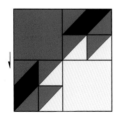

Make 56.

ASSEMBLING AND FINISHING THE QUILT TOP

1. Arrange the blocks in eight rows of seven blocks each, rotating every other block as shown in the quilt assembly diagram.

2. Sew the blocks into rows. Press the seam allowances in alternate directions from row to row. Sew the rows together. Press the seam allowances in one direction.

3. Refer to "Adding Borders" on page 43. Measure, cut, and sew the 1½"-wide fabric C strips to the quilt top for the inner border, and then the 4½"-wide fabric D strips for the outer border. Press all seam allowances toward the newly added borders.

4. Layer the quilt with batting and the pieced backing; baste. Hand or machine quilt as desired.

5. Refer to "Binding Your Quilt" on page 44 and use the 2½"-wide fabric D strips to bind the quilt.

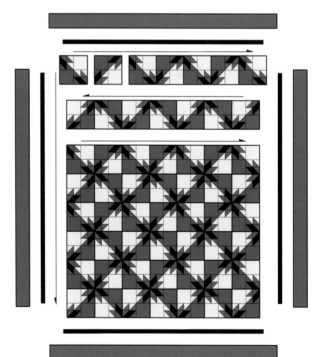

Quilt assembly

Pieced and quilted by Jo Parrott

This 10" Hunter's Star block is great for beginning quilters who want to work with pieces larger than the 8" blocks in "Shimmering Hunter's Star" on page 20. The blocks are assembled in the same manner, forming arrows and stars. The beauty of using larger blocks is that you can make the same size quilt with fewer blocks.

Finished quilt: 68½" x 88½"
Finished block: 10"

MATERIALS

All yardages are based on 42"-wide fabric.
3⅛ yards of fabric A (dark purple) for arrows and binding
2⅜ yards of fabric B (light green) for arrows
2⅓ yards of fabric C (light purple) for stars and border
1¼ yards of fabric D (dark green) for stars
5¾ yards of fabric for backing
74" x 94" piece of batting

CUTTING

All measurements include ¼"-wide seam allowances. Cut all strips across the width of the fabric (selvage to selvage). Read all the directions before starting, referring to "Special Techniques" on page 7 as needed.

From fabric A, cut:
1 strip, 15" x 42"; crosscut into 2 rectangles, 15" x 20"
2 strips, 12" x 42"; crosscut into 4 rectangles, 12" x 20"
7 strips, 5½" x 42"; crosscut into 48 squares, 5½" x 5½"
9 strips, 2½" x 42"

From fabric B, cut:
1 strip, 15" x 42"; crosscut into 2 rectangles, 15" x 20"
2 strips, 12" x 42"; crosscut into 4 rectangles, 12" x 20"
7 strips, 5½" x 42"; crosscut into 48 squares, 5½" x 5½"

From fabric C, cut:
1 strip, 15" x 42"; crosscut into 2 rectangles, 15" x 20"
2 strips, 12" x 42"; crosscut into 4 rectangles, 12" x 20"
8 strips, 4½" x 42"

From fabric D, cut:
1 strip, 15" x 42"; crosscut into 2 rectangles, 15" x 20"
2 strips, 12" x 42"; crosscut into 4 rectangles, 12" x 20"

Color Swatch

Even though this quilt uses only four fabrics, the fabrics are used in different places in the block, which can become confusing. So, for easy reference, I find it handy to cut a swatch of each of my fabrics and either pin them or paste them with fabric glue to a sheet of paper. I then label each swatch as fabric A, B, C, or D to help me keep on track as I'm cutting and sewing my quilt pieces

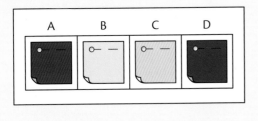

MAKING THE HALF-SQUARE-TRIANGLE UNITS

Refer to "Half-Square-Triangle Grid Technique" on page 7 for details.

1. Layer the 15" x 20" rectangles in pairs, right sides together, with the lighter fabric on top in the following combinations:
   - Fabric A and fabric C
   - Fabric A and fabric B
   - Fabric B and fabric D
   - Fabric C and fabric D
2. Draw a 3⅜" grid on the wrong side of each top rectangle. Sew the rectangles together as described in "Half-Square-Triangle Grid Technique." Make one of each combination of fabrics. Cut on the lines to make 40 half-square-triangle units from each fabric combination. Press the seam allowances toward fabrics A and D. Each half-square-triangle unit should measure 3" square.

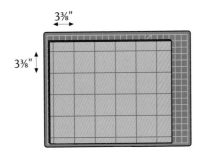

3. Repeat steps 1 and 2 using the 12" x 20" rectangles. Make two of each combination of fabrics. Cut 56 half-square-triangle units from each fabric combination. (You'll have four extra half-square-triangle units from each fabric combination for your scrap bag.)

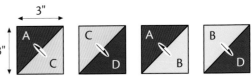

Make 96 of each.

MAKING THE BLOCKS

1. Sew an A/C half-square-triangle unit and a C/D half-square-triangle unit together as shown; press. Make 48 units.

Make 48.

2. Sew an A/B half-square-triangle unit and a D/B half-square-triangle unit together as shown; press. Make 48 units.

Make 48.

3. Sew one unit from step 1 and one unit from step 2 together to make a unit that measures 5½" square; press. Make 48 units.

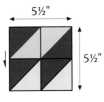

Make 48.

4. Sew a fabric A square to the left side of the unit from step 3. Press the seam allowances toward fabric A. Make 48 units.

Make 48.

5. Sew an A/C half-square-triangle unit and an A/B half-square-triangle unit together as shown; press. Make 48 units.

Make 48.

6. Sew a C/D half-square-triangle unit and a D/B half-square-triangle unit together as shown; press. Make 48 units.

Make 48.

7. Sew one unit from step 5 and one unit from step 6 together to make a unit that measures 5½" square; press. Make 48 units.

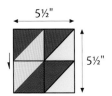

5½"

5½"

Make 48.

8. Sew a fabric B square to the right side of the unit from step 7. Press the seam allowances toward fabric B. Make 48 units.

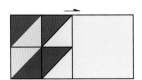

Make 48.

9. Sew one unit from step 4 and one unit from step 8 together as shown to make one block; press. Make 48 blocks.

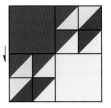

Make 48.

ASSEMBLING AND FINISHING THE QUILT TOP

1. Arrange the blocks in eight rows of six blocks each, rotating every other block as shown in the quilt assembly diagram.
2. Sew the blocks into rows. Press the seam allowances in alternate directions from row to row. Sew the rows together. Press the seam allowances in one direction.
3. Refer to "Adding Borders" on page 43. Measure, cut, sew, and press the 4½"-wide fabric C strips to the quilt top for the outer border.
4. Layer the quilt with batting and the pieced backing; baste. Hand or machine quilt as desired.
5. Refer to "Binding Your Quilt" on page 44 and use the 2½"-wide fabric A strips to bind the quilt.

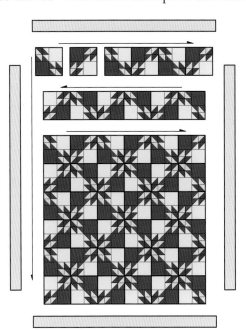

Quilt assembly

Twinkling Hunter's Star

It's always fun to see how the choice of fabric and color can completely change the character of a quilt design. In this version, I've exchanged the primary colors of the "Shimmering Hunter's Star" for a palette of cool colors with less contrast for a dramatically different effect.

Finished size: 66½" x 74½"

Pieced and quilted by Jo Parrott

In this version, the dark pink arrows take center stage, while the stars recede. A wide dark pink inner border frames the blocks and draws your eye to the center of the quilt.

Finished size: 78" x 86"

*Made in honor of Marie Tannahill Thompson by
Billie Sanders Thompson. Quilted by Karen Denny.*

Pieced and quilted by Jo Parrott

The Mock Log Cabin block is called "mock" because it's made with fewer strips than a traditional Log Cabin; therefore it's much faster to make, yet it can be arranged in any setting typically used for a traditional Log Cabin quilt. The block has a diagonal separation of color. I used the Barn Raising setting, but you could use the Streak of Lightning or Straight Furrows setting shown on pages 38 and 40, or any arrangement you like.

Finished quilt: 80½" x 80½"
Finished block: 8"

MATERIALS

All yardages are based on 42"-wide fabric.
3⅝ yards of pink fabric for blocks
2¼ yards of green fabric for blocks and binding
2 yards dark gray fabric for blocks
1¼ yards of red fabric for blocks
1¼ yards of floral print for blocks
7⅞ yards of fabric for backing
86" x 86" piece of batting

CUTTING

All measurements include ¼"-wide seam allowances.
Cut all strips across the width of the fabric (selvage to selvage). Read all the directions before starting, referring to "Special Techniques" on page 7 as needed.

From the dark gray fabric, cut:
25 strips, 2½" x 42"; crosscut into 400 squares, 2½" x 2½"

From the pink fabric, cut:
7 strips, 8½" x 42"; crosscut into 100 rectangles, 2½" x 8½"
13 strips, 4½" x 42"; crosscut into 200 rectangles, 2½" x 4½"

From the floral print, cut:
2 strips, 8½" x 42"; crosscut into 32 rectangles, 2½" x 8½"
4 strips, 4½" x 42"; crosscut into 64 rectangles, 2½" x 4½"

From the red fabric, cut:
2 strips, 8½" x 42"; crosscut into 32 rectangles, 2½" x 8½"
4 strips, 4½" x 42"; crosscut into 64 rectangles, 2½" x 4½"

From the green fabric, cut:
3 strips, 8½" x 42"; crosscut into 36 rectangles, 2½" x 8½"
5 strips, 4½" x 42"; crosscut into 72 rectangles, 2½" x 4½"
9 strips, 2½" x 42"

MAKING THE BLOCKS

1. Using the "Corner Triangles" technique on page 11, draw a diagonal line from corner to corner on the wrong side of the 2½" gray squares. Sew a marked square on one end of each 2½" x 8½" pink rectangle as shown. Trim the outer corner of the square, leaving the bottom rectangle intact. Flip open the remaining triangle and press. Make 100 pink units. Repeat to make 32 units using the 2½" x 8½" floral rectangles, 32 units using the 2½" x 8½" red rectangles, and 36 units using the 2½" x 8½" green rectangles.

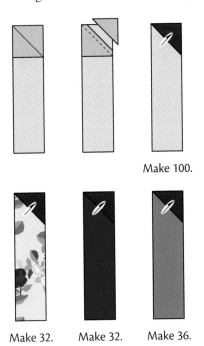

Make 100.

Make 32.   Make 32.   Make 36.

2. Repeat step 1 using the remaining gray squares and the 2½" x 4½" pink, floral, red, and green rectangles. Make 100 pink, 32 floral, 32 red, and 36 green units.

Make 100.   Make 32.   Make 32.   Make 36.

3. Sew a 2½" x 4½" pink rectangle to one side of each pink unit from step 2, making sure to position the pieces as shown; press. Make 100 pink units.

Make 100.

4. Repeat step 3, sewing each unit from step 2 and a 2½" x 4½" matching rectangle together; press. Make 32 floral, 32 red, and 36 green units.

Make 32.   Make 32.   Make 36.

5. Sew one unit from step 3 to each unit from step 4 as shown; press.

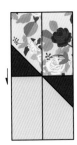

6. Sew one unit from step 5 between one pink unit from step 1 and a floral, red, or green unit from step 1 as shown; press. Make 32 floral/pink blocks, 32 red/pink blocks, and 36 green/pink blocks.

Make 32.   Make 32.   Make 36.

ASSEMBLING AND FINISHING THE QUILT TOP

1. Arrange the blocks in ten rows of ten blocks each, rotating every other block as shown in the quilt assembly diagram.

2. Sew the blocks into rows. Press the seam allowances in alternate directions from row to row. Sew the rows together. Press the seam allowances in one direction.

3. Baste around the quilt top about ⅛" from the outer edge to stabilize the seams, being careful not to stretch the seams as you sew.

4. Layer the quilt with batting and the pieced backing; baste. Hand or machine quilt as desired.

5. Refer to "Binding Your Quilt" on page 44 and use the 2½"-wide green strips to bind the quilt.

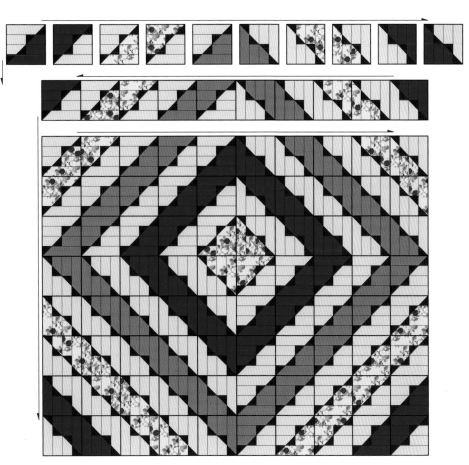

Quilt assembly

Pieced and quilted by Jo Parrott

The Modified Nine Patch is such a versatile block. It's easy to make, but when it is assembled, it looks like a more difficult pattern. The blocks can be set together in so many ways. This quilt and "Casey's Nine Patch" on page 38 are made with the same number of 6" blocks, but look entirely different.

Finished quilt: 60½" x 84½"
Finished block: 6"

MATERIALS

All yardages are based on 42"-wide fabric.
3⅝ yards *total* of assorted dark scraps for blocks
3 yards *total* of assorted light scraps for blocks
⅔ yard of fabric for binding
5½ yards of fabric for backing
66" x 90" piece of batting

Fabric Selection Tip

The Modified Nine Patch blocks are made from scraps. You will need a variety of light (including white and/or cream) prints and dark prints of any shade. Before you start sewing the blocks, cut the squares and stack them in four different containers. Label each container with the color, square size, and number needed.

CUTTING

All measurements include ¼"-wide seam allowances. Cut all strips across the width of the fabric (selvage to selvage). Read all the directions before starting, referring to "Special Techniques" on page 7 as needed.

From the assorted dark scraps, cut a *total* of:
140 squares, 2⅞" x 2⅞"
560 squares, 2½" x 2½"

From the assorted light scraps, cut a *total* of:
140 squares, 2⅞" x 2⅞"
420 squares, 2½" x 2½"

From the binding fabric, cut:
8 strips, 2½" x 42"

Making the Blocks

1. Using the "Scrap Half-Square-Triangle Units" technique on page 10, sew each 2⅞" light square and 2⅞" dark square together as described. Make 280 half-square-triangle units.

Make 280.

2. Arrange two half-square-triangle units, four 2½" dark squares, and three 2½" light squares as shown. Sew the squares into rows; press. Sew the rows together to complete the block; press. Make 140 blocks total.

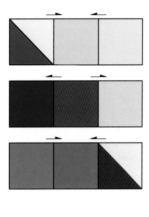

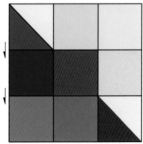

Make 140.

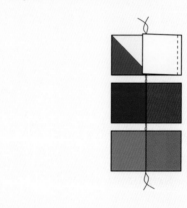

Sewing Tip

I like to assembly-line (or chain) stitch the squares together. To do this I sew the first pair of squares together, and then without lifting the presser foot or cutting the thread, I sew the next pair of squares together. When I've stitched pairs of squares for 10–12 blocks, I clip the thread after the last pair and remove the pieces from the machine. Don't clip the thread between the squares yet. Then I feed the squares under the presser foot again, adding the third square in each row as shown.

Assembling and Finishing the Quilt Top

1. Arrange the blocks in 14 rows of 10 blocks each. You'll need seven each of row A and row B. Notice that in row A, the blocks are rotated from one block to the next but that the dark edge of the block is always along the top of the row. In row B, the light portion of the block is always along the top of the row. Sew the blocks together in rows. Press the seam allowances in alternate directions from row to row.

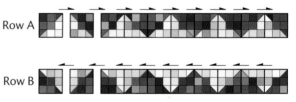

Row A

Row B

Make 7 of each.

2. Stitch the rows together and press the seam allowances in one direction.

3. Baste around the quilt top about ⅛" from the outer edge to stabilize the seams, being careful not to stretch the seams as you sew.

4. Layer the quilt top with batting and the pieced backing; baste. Hand or machine quilt as desired.

5. Refer to "Binding Your Quilt" on page 44 and use the 2½"-wide binding strips to bind the quilt.

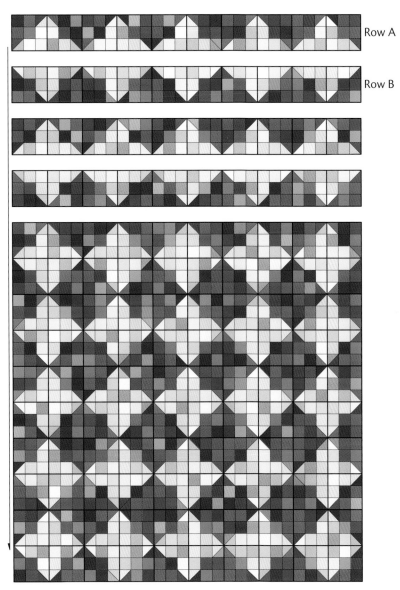

Row A

Row B

Quilt assembly

Pieced and quilted by Jo Parrott

What a versatile block! In this quilt, I used the same Modified Nine Patch block as in "Nine Patch Jewels" on page 34, yet the quilt has a completely different look. I used the same size and number of blocks as before, but here I limited my fabric selections. Instead of using all the colors in my scrap bag, I limited the dark prints to shades of green and the light fabrics are primarily creams and off-whites. To put it all together, I set the blocks in a zigzag or Streak of Lightning design.

Finished quilt: 60½" x 84½"
Finished block: 6"

MATERIALS

All yardages are based on 42"-wide fabric.
3⅝ yards *total* of assorted medium and dark green scraps for blocks
3 yards *total* of assorted light scraps for blocks
⅔ yard of fabric for binding
5½ yards of fabric for backing
66" x 90" piece of batting

Add a Border

To make your quilt larger, you can simply add a border. For example, to make a 71" x 95" quilt, you'll need 1½ yards of fabric. From the border fabric, cut eight strips, 6" x 42".

CUTTING

All measurements include ¼"-wide seam allowances. Cut all strips across the width of the fabric (selvage to selvage). Read all the directions before starting, referring to "Special Techniques" on page 7 as needed.

From the assorted medium and dark green scraps, cut a *total* of:
140 squares, 2⅞" x 2⅞"
560 squares, 2½" x 2½"

From the assorted light scraps, cut a *total* of:
140 squares, 2⅞" x 2⅞"
420 squares, 2½" x 2½"

From the binding fabric, cut:
8 strips, 2½" x 42"

MAKING THE BLOCKS

1. Using the "Scrap Half-Square-Triangle Units" technique on page 10, sew each 2⅞" light square and 2⅞" green square together as described. Cut the squares apart and press open to make 280 half-square-triangle units.

Make 280.

2. Arrange two half-square-triangle units, four 2½" green squares, and three 2½" light squares as shown. Sew the squares into rows; press. Sew the rows together to complete the block and press. Make 140 total.

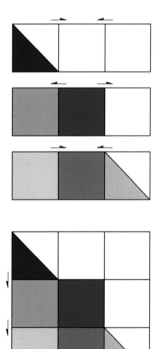

Make 140.

Setting and Size Options

As I've mentioned, the Modified Nine Patch is truly a versatile quilt block. Because the block features a diagonal split of the dark and light colors, you can use this block in any quilt setting that's suitable for another all-purpose block, the Log Cabin. Zigzag, Sunshine and Shadow, Straight Furrows, and more are fun ways to set these quilt blocks. So before you set your mind on a specific setting, I recommend playing around with different options. The possibilities are just about endless.

Straight Furrows (140 blocks)

Barn Raising (144 blocks)

ASSEMBLING AND FINISHING THE QUILT TOP

1. Arrange the blocks in 14 rows of 10 blocks each. Notice that the blocks are turned so that the green portion slants one way in row A blocks and the opposite direction in row B blocks. You'll need seven each of row A and row B.

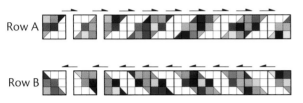

Make 7 of each.

2. Sew the blocks together in rows. Press the seam allowances in alternate directions from row to row. Stitch the rows together and press the seam allowances in one direction.
3. Baste around the quilt top about ⅛" from the outer edge to stabilize the seams, being careful not to stretch the seams as you sew.
4. Layer the quilt top with batting and the backing; baste. Hand or machine quilt as desired.
5. Refer to "Binding Your Quilt" on page 44 and use the 2½"-wide binding strips to bind the quilt.

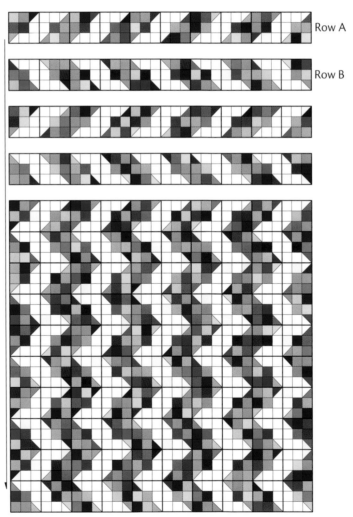

Quilt assembly

Once the blocks are completed, you'll need to decide if you want to add borders. Then you can finish the quilt, which includes piecing the backing, layering and basting the layers, quilting, and finally applying the binding. The following instructions will help you with adding borders and binding your quilt.

ADDING BORDERS

The projects in this book provide examples of borderless quilts and quilts with simple borders. Don't forget the importance of the borders, which often frame or finish the quilt. A beautifully pieced top can become an off-centered, uneven quilt if the borders are not added correctly. The main objective is to keep the quilt square so that it hangs straight and lies flat.

The quilts in this book that include borders call for plain border strips. The strips are cut crosswise selvage to selvage and joined end to end with a diagonal or straight seam where extra length is needed. There is a slight give in the fabric when the strips are cut in this manner, but it takes less fabric than when you cut strips from the lengthwise grain (parallel to the selvage).

I have not given any measurements for cutting your border-strip lengths. These measurements are determined once your quilt top is put together, as described in the border method that follows.

1. Measure the length of the quilt in three places. If the measurements are not all the same, average them. For example, if the three measurements are 88½", 88¾", and 89", the average would be 88¾". Cut two strips the length determined for the side borders, piecing as necessary.

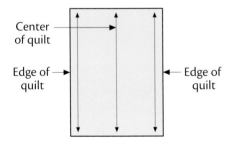

Measure in three places, top to bottom.

2. Mark the center of the quilt edges and border strips. Pin the borders to the sides of the quilt top, matching the centers and ends. Ease or slightly stretch the quilt top to fit the border strips as necessary. Sew the side borders in place with a ¼"-wide seam allowance and press the seam allowances toward the border strips. (I sew with the borders on the bottom to make sure all the seam allowances fall in the intended direction.)

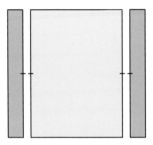

Mark centers.

3. Measure the width of the quilt in three places (including the just-added borders) and determine the average. Cut two strips to this measurement, piecing as necessary. Mark the center of the quilt edges and border strips. Pin the borders to the quilt top, matching the centers and ends, and sew them in place. Press the seam allowances toward the border strips.

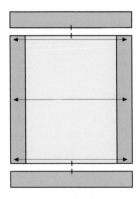

Measure in three places, side to side. Mark centers.

QUILTING

All quilts in this book have been quilted on a long-arm quilting machine. Check with the quilter before preparing your finished quilt top and backing to determine the correct size of backing needed, and leave layering to the professional quilter. If you plan to quilt by hand or on your home sewing machine, the quilt top, batting, and backing will need to be layered and basted together before quilting.

BINDING YOUR QUILT

All the bindings for the quilts in this book were cut 2½" wide across the width of fabric and pieced. Machine baste around the edges about ⅛" from the edge of the quilt top. Trim the batting and backing so that it extends about 1" beyond the edges of the quilt top on all sides.

1. Cut strips as specified in the cutting directions for your quilt.

2. To make one long, continuous strip, piece the strips at right angles and stitch across the corner as shown. Trim the excess fabric, leaving a ¼"-wide seam allowance, and press the seam allowances open.

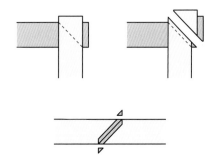

3. Cut one end of the long binding strip at a 45° angle and turn under ¼" as shown. Press the strip in half lengthwise, wrong sides together and raw edges aligned.

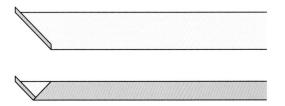

4. Beginning with the angled end of the binding strip, align the raw edge of the strip with the raw edge of the quilt top. Starting on one side (not in a corner) and beginning 3" from the angled end, use a walking foot and a ¼"-wide seam allowance to stitch the binding to the quilt. Stop ¼" from the first corner and backstitch.

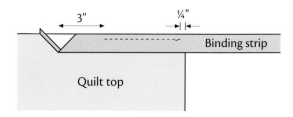

5. Remove the quilt from the sewing machine. Fold the binding straight up and away from the quilt so the fold forms a 45° angle.

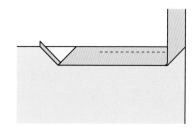

6. Fold the binding back down onto itself, even with the edge of the quilt top, to create an angled pleat at the corner and pin in place. Begin with a backstitch at the fold of the binding and continue stitching along the edge of the quilt top, mitering each corner as you come to it.

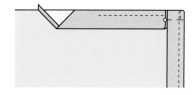

7. Stop stitching approximately 3" from the starting end of the binding strip and backstitch. Remove the quilt from the machine. Trim the binding tail 1" longer than needed and tuck the end inside the beginning of the strip. Pin in place, making sure the strip lies flat. Then finish

stitching the binding to the quilt top. Trim the excess batting and backing even with the quilt top.

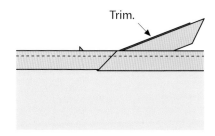

Trim.

8. Turn the binding to the back of the quilt. Using thread to match the binding, hand stitch the binding in place so that the folded edge covers the row of machine stitching. At each corner, fold the binding to form a miter on the back of the quilt.

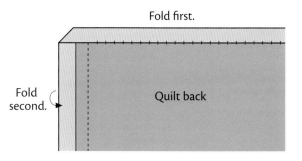

Fold first.

Fold second.

Quilt back

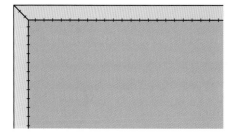

SIGNING YOUR QUILT

Future generations will want to know who made your quilt. A label provides important information, including the name of the quilt, who made it, when it was made, and where. You may also want to include the name of the recipient, if it's a gift, and any other interesting or important information about the quilt.

You can stabilize your label fabric by ironing a piece of freezer paper to the wrong side. Use a fine-tipped permanent fabric pen to record the information on the fabric, and then remove the freezer paper. Attach it to the back of the quilt with small stitches.

Jo Parrott began quilting in 1982, and has made over 500 quilts since that time. She likes to take traditional quilts and make them easier to assemble. The great joys of her life are her 23 grandchildren, 10 great grandchildren, and her quilting students. Jo and her husband, Henry, owned a quilt shop in Dallas, Not Just Quilts, for six years, and presently live in East Texas in a home they built themselves. When Jo kept stacking up quilt tops that needed to be quilted, Henry decided to try his hand at making a long-arm quilting machine for her. This was successful, and Jo quilted 49 quilts the first year she had it.

Acknowledgments

Many thanks to Carroll Moore, Alice Wilson, and Billie Thompson at the Country Junction Quilt Store in Wills Point, Texas, and to everyone at Martingale & Company, the home of That Patchwork Place, for their hard work, encouragement, and support.

A special thank you to Henry, my husband, for his support and for building me my own quilting machine.

New and Bestselling Titles from

America's Best-Loved
Quilt Books®

America's Best-Loved Craft & Hobby Books®
America's Best-Loved Knitting Books®

APPLIQUÉ
Appliqué Quilt Revival—*NEW!*
Beautiful Blooms
Cutting-Garden Quilts
More Fabulous Flowers—*NEW!*
Sunbonnet Sue and Scottie Too

BABIES AND CHILDREN
Baby Wraps
Lickety-Split Quilts for Little Ones
The Little Box of Baby Quilts
Snuggle-and-Learn Quilts for Kids—*NEW!*
Sweet and Simple Baby Quilts

BEGINNER
Color for the Terrified Quilter
Happy Endings, Revised Edition
Let's Quilt!
Machine Appliqué for the Terrified Quilter
Your First Quilt Book (or it should be!)

GENERAL QUILTMAKING
Adventures in Circles—*NEW!*
Bits and Pieces
Charmed
Cool Girls Quilt
Country-Fresh Quilts—*NEW!*
Creating Your Perfect Quilting Space
Creative Quilt Collection Volume Three
A Dozen Roses
Follow-the-Line Quilting Designs
    Volume Three
Gathered from the Garden—*NEW!*
Points of View
Positively Postcards
Prairie Children and Their Quilts
Quilt Revival
A Quilter's Diary
Quilter's Happy Hour
Simple Seasons
Skinny Quilts and Table Runners
Twice Quilted
Young at Heart Quilts

HOLIDAY AND SEASONAL
Christmas with Artful Offerings
Christmas Quilts from Hopscotch—*NEW!*
Comfort and Joy
Holiday Wrappings—*NEW!*

HOOKED RUGS, NEEDLE FELTING, AND PUNCHNEEDLE
The Americana Collection
Miniature Punchneedle Embroidery
Needle-Felting Magic
Needle Felting with Cotton and Wool
Punchneedle Fun

PAPER PIECING
300 Paper-Pieced Quilt Blocks
A Year of Paper Piecing—*NEW!*
Paper-Pieced Mini Quilts
Show Me How to Paper Piece
Showstopping Quilts to Foundation Piece

PIECING
Copy Cat Quilts
Maple Leaf Quilts
Mosaic Picture Quilts
New Cuts for New Quilts
Nine by Nine
On-Point Quilts—*NEW!*
Ribbon Star Quilts
Rolling Along
Quiltastic Curves
Sew One and You're Done
Square Deal
Sudoku Quilts

QUICK QUILTS
40 Fabulous Quick-Cut Quilts
Instant Bargello—*NEW!*
Quilts on the Double
Sew Fun, So Colorful Quilts
Wonder Blocks

SCRAP QUILTS
Nickel Quilts
Save the Scraps
Simple Strategies for Scrap Quilts
Spotlight on Scraps

CRAFTS
Art from the Heart
The Beader's Handbook
Card Design
Creative Embellishments
Crochet for Beaders
Dolly Mama Beads—*NEW!*
Friendship Bracelets All Grown Up—*NEW!*
It's a Wrap
The Little Box of Beaded Bracelets
    and Earrings
Sculpted Threads
Sew Sentimental

KNITTING & CROCHET
365 Crochet Stitches a Year:
    Perpetual Calendar
365 Knitting Stitches a Year:
    Perpetual Calendar
A to Z of Knitting
Amigurumi World
Cable Confidence
Casual, Elegant Knits—*NEW!*
Chic Knits
Crocheted Pursenalities
First Knits
Gigi Knits…and Purls—*NEW!*
Kitty Knits
The Knitter's Book of Finishing Techniques
Knitting Circles around Socks
Knitting with Gigi
Modern Classics
More Sensational Knitted Socks
Pursenalities
Simple Gifts for Dog Lovers
Skein for Skein—*NEW!*

Our books are available at bookstores and your favorite craft, fabric, and yarn retailers. If you don't see the title you're looking for, visit us at www.martingale-pub.com or contact us at:

1-800-426-3126

International: 1-425-483-3313
Fax: 1-425-486-7596 • Email: info@martingale-pub.com

6/08